Learn With Images
Chinese / English

Kàn tú xuéxí

看 图 学习

Zhōngwén / Yīngwén

中文 / 英文

Yinka Amuda

authorHOUSE®

AuthorHouse™
1663 Liberty Drive
Bloomington, IN 47403
www.authorhouse.com
Phone: 1-800-839-8640

Published by AuthorHouse   04/01/2013

ISBN: 978-1-4817-8856-4 (sc)
ISBN: 978-1-4817-8857-1 (e)

Edited by:

Debo Amuda
Chun Tsua
Liang Jyun

For Service & Smiles Company

练习1 朋友

Exercise 1/liànxíyī - Friends/yŏu

Zhèliǎnggènánháizhīqiánzhèngzàihéduìfāngchǎojià

1. 这2个男孩之前正在和对方吵架。
   The two boys were quarrelling with each other.
   先前，这2个男孩正在吵架。

Zhègenǔháihézhègenánháicéngjīngzàihēi'ànzhōnghùxiāngyǐndǎo.

2. 这个女孩和这个男孩曾经在黑暗中互相引导。
   The girl and the boy guided each other in the dark.

Màndìcéngshìgèměilì de nǔháishòudàotāsuǒyǒupéngyǒu de chŏng'ài

3. 蔓蒂曾是个美丽的女孩受到她所有朋友的宠爱。
   Mandy was a beautiful girl who was loved by all her friends.

Nǐyīnggāichángshìzàinǐwǒzhījiānbǎoshǒuzhègemìmì

4. 你应该尝试在你我之间保守这个秘密。
   You should try to keep this secret between you and me.
   你应该尽量保守这个秘密。

Báiqí·fùlánkèlíncéngjīnggàosuguòtāyàolìkèguīhuánzhèzhīgāngbǐ

5. 白琦·富兰克林曾经告诉过他要立刻归还这支钢笔。
   Becky frankly told him to return the fountain pen immediately.
   白琦·富兰克林曾经告诉他要立刻归还这支钢笔

Jiémǔsībùhuìgēnwǒlái,

sàlāyěbùhuì.

6.　杰姆斯不会跟我来，萨拉也不会

。

Neither James nor Sarah is coming

with me.

练习2-家

Exercise 2/liànxíèr – Home/zhái

	Tācéngjīngbǎnǔwáng de túxiàngguàzàiwū li
	1. 她曾经把女王的图像挂在屋里。
	She hung the pictures of the queen in the house.
	Zhègecéngjīngtǎngzàizhuōshàng de zhōngzhīqiánbèinònghuàile
	2. 这个曾经躺在桌上的钟之前被弄坏了。
	The clock which was lying on the table was destroyed.
	曾放在桌上的钟是已被弄坏的。
	Zhǐyàonǐyuànyìnǐkěyǐyòngzhègechábēi
	3. 只要你愿意你可以用这个茶杯。
	You may use this cup as long as you want.
	Yīgènǔshìzàitā de jiātínggōngzuòzhōngyīdìngyàozǐxì.
	4. 一个女士在她的家庭工作中一定要仔细。
	A lady must be careful in her domestic work.
	女士做家务时一定要小心谨慎。
	Yīgèrénkěyǐbiǎoxiàn de jiùxiàngzhègerénzàizìjǐjiālǐyīyàng
	5. 一个人可以表现得就像这个人在自己家里一样。
	One can behave as one likes in one's own home.
	一个人可以表现的像他在自己的家一样。

Tābùdànzàoleyīdòngfángziháizàoleyīgèchēkù

6. 他不但造了一栋房子还造了一个车库。

He not only built a house but also a garage.

他不但盖了一栋房子还盖了一个车库。

"Nàgèzhèngzàiqiāowǒmén de rénshìshuí?"Shìjiékè, nǚshì."

7. '那个正在敲我门的人是谁？' '是杰克，女士。'

'Who is that knocking at my door?' 'It's Jack, madam.'

谁在敲我家的门？' '是杰克，女士。

练习3-饮食

Exercise 3/liànxísān – Food/yǐnshí

	Tāměitiāndōuhēpútáojiǔ 1. 她每天都喝葡萄酒。 She drinks wine every day.
	Zhèxiēnánfúwùyuánzàizhāodàidiǎnxīnshíyǒuz heshēhuá de guīmó. 2. 这些男服务员在招待点心时有着奢华的规模 。 The waiters partook of the refreshments served on a lavish scale. 这些上点心的服务员非常慷慨，供应丰富 。
	Tāláizhīqiánwǒjiùyǐjīngchīlezǎofàn. 3. 他来之前我就已经吃了早饭。 I had taken my breakfast before he came.
	Yīgèrénbùnéngxǐhuanchīshénmejiùchīshé nme 4. 一个人不能喜欢吃什么就吃什么。 One cannot eat what one likes.
	Zhègeyǐnshìcéngjīngkàoshuǐguǒdùrì. 5. 这个隐士曾经靠水果度日。 The hermit had to subsist on fruits.

Exercise 3/liànxísān – Food/yǐnshí

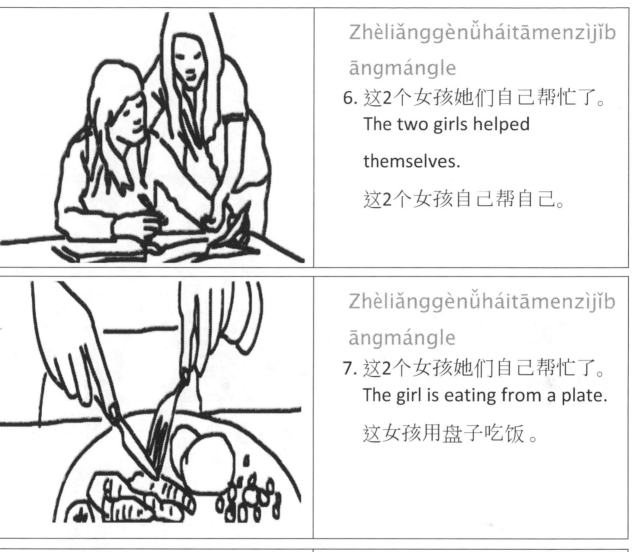

Zhèliǎnggènǚháitāmenzìjǐb
āngmángle

6. 这2个女孩她们自己帮忙了。
The two girls helped

themselves.

这2个女孩自己帮自己。

Zhèliǎnggènǚháitāmenzìjǐb
āngmángle

7. 这2个女孩她们自己帮忙了。
The girl is eating from a plate.

这女孩用盘子吃饭 。

Tāwèntāmenzhèngzàichīsh
énme

8. 她问他们正在吃什么。
She asked them what they

were eating.

练习4-意见

Exercise 4/liànxísì – Opinion/yánlùn

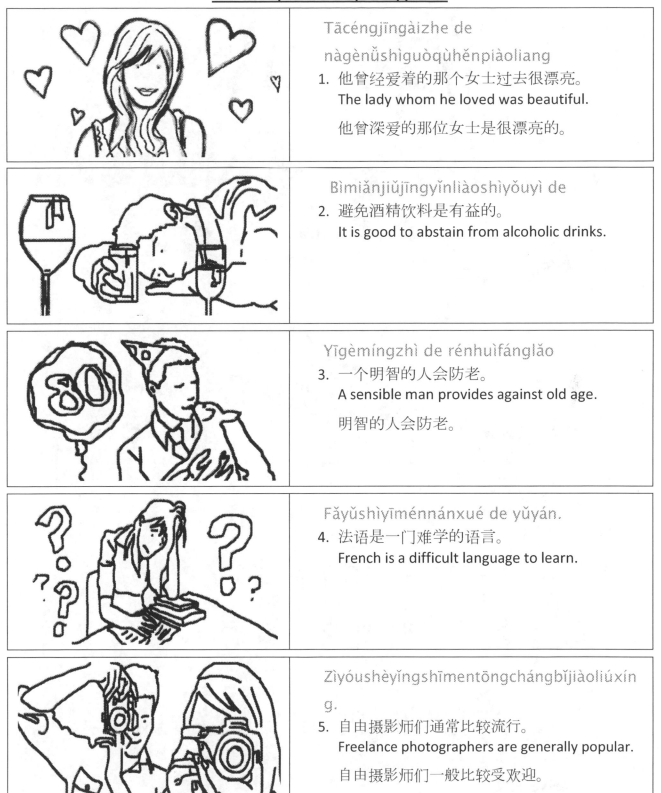

Tācéngjīngàizhe de
nàgènǚshìguòqùhěnpiàoliang
1. 他曾经爱着的那个女士过去很漂亮。
   The lady whom he loved was beautiful.

   他曾深爱的那位女士是很漂亮的。

Bìmiǎnjiǔjīngyǐnliàoshìyǒuyì de
2. 避免酒精饮料是有益的。
   It is good to abstain from alcoholic drinks.

Yīgèmíngzhì de rénhuìfánglǎo
3. 一个明智的人会防老。
   A sensible man provides against old age.

   明智的人会防老。

Fǎyǔshìyīménnánxué de yǔyán.
4. 法语是一门难学的语言。
   French is a difficult language to learn.

Zìyóushèyǐngshīmentōngchángbǐjiàoliúxíng.
5. 自由摄影师们通常比较流行。
   Freelance photographers are generally popular.

   自由摄影师们一般比较受欢迎。

Wǒyīnggāibèishādiào,
méiyǒurénjiānghuìjiùwǒ

6.　我应该被杀掉，没有人将会救我。

I shall be killed and nobody will save me.

练习5-金钱

Exercise 5/liànxíwǔ – Money/bì

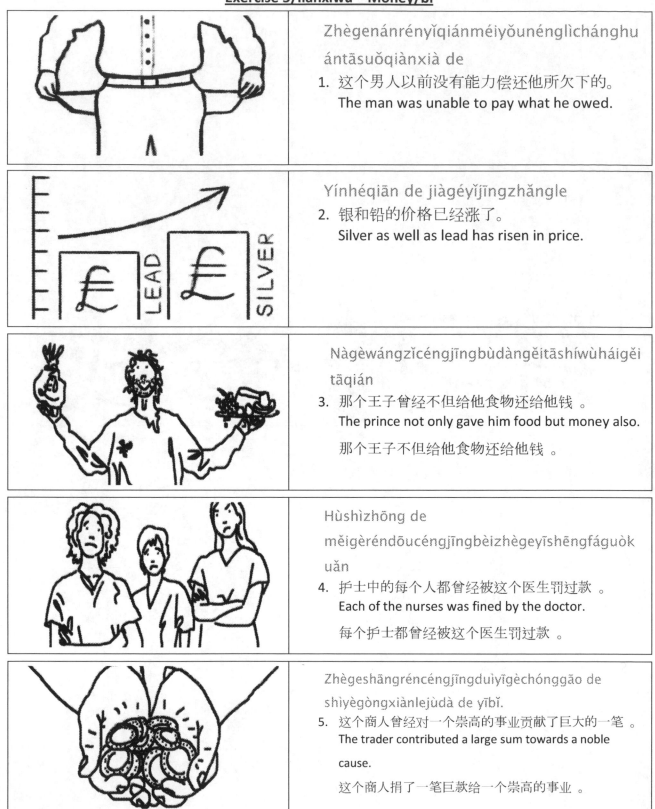

Zhègenánrényǐqiánméiyǒunénglìchánghuántāsuǒqiànxià de

1. 这个男人以前没有能力偿还他所欠下的。
   The man was unable to pay what he owed.

Yínhéqiān de jiàgéyǐjīngzhǎngle

2. 银和铅的价格已经涨了。
   Silver as well as lead has risen in price.

Nàgèwángzǐcéngjīngbùdàngěitāshíwùháigěitāqián

3. 那个王子曾经不但给他食物还给他钱 。
   The prince not only gave him food but money also.

   那个王子不但给他食物还给他钱 。

Hùshìzhōng de měigèréndōucéngjīngbèizhègeyīshēngfáguòkuǎn

4. 护士中的每个人都曾经被这个医生罚过款 。
   Each of the nurses was fined by the doctor.

   每个护士都曾经被这个医生罚过款 。

Zhègeshāngréncéngjīngduìyīgèchónggāo de shìyègòngxiànlejùdà de yībǐ.

5. 这个商人曾经对一个崇高的事业贡献了巨大的一笔 。
   The trader contributed a large sum towards a noble cause.

   这个商人捐了一笔巨款给一个崇高的事业 。

Wǔbǎibàngduìzhègexiàngmùbùgòu

6.　　五百镑对这个项目不够 。

Five hundred pounds is not enough for

the project.

这项目超过500磅

练习6-旅游

Exercise 6/liànxíliù – Travel/lǚyóu

	Zhègenǚháicéngjīngchángshìguòhěnkuài fǎnhuí 1. 这个女孩曾经尝试过很快返回。 The girl tried to return quickly. 这个女孩曾试过要尽快返回。
	Kèlǐsītuōfú · gēlúnbùfāxiànleměizhōu 2. 克里斯托弗·哥伦布发现了美洲。 Christopher Columbus discovered America.
	Zhègelǚxíngjiābèixiǎotōumendiàosǐle 3. 这个旅行家被小偷们吊死了。 The traveller was hanged by the thieves.
	Zhègemòshēngrényǒuběnshìshǐzìjǐshìyìnghuán jìng. 4. 这个陌生人有本事使自己适应环境。 The stranger has the power to adapt himself to circumstances. 这个陌生人适应环境的能力很强 。
	Sìshíyīnglǐbùshìyīduànduǎnjùlí. 5. 四十英里不是一段短距离。 Forty miles is not a short distance.

Zàiwǒlái de shíhoujiùbǎzhègexínglǐzhǔnbèihǎo

6. 在我来的时候就把这个行李准备好。
Get the luggage ready for my arrival.

Zhèliàngchēbǎochíjìngzhǐyǒusāngèyuèle

7. 这辆车保持静止有三个月了。
The car remained stationary for three months.

这辆车已有三个月没开动过了。

Zhèsōutǐngyǐqiánshìhuài de.

8. 这艘艇以前是坏的。
The boat was broken up.

这艘船已坏的。

练习7-比较

Exercise 7/liànxíqī – Comparison/yìtóng

	Zhèshìkǎdífuzuìgǔlǎo de jiànzhú 1. 这是卡迪夫最古老的建筑。 This is the oldest building in Cardiff.
	Zàisuǒyǒu de jiàshǐyuándāngzhōngtāshìzuìhǎo de. 2. 在所有的驾驶员当中他是最好的。 Of all the drivers he is the best.
	Wǒ de gēgēhéjiejieyīyàngyǒushàn 3. 我的哥哥和姐姐一样友善。 My brother as well as my sister is kind. 我的哥哥还有我姐姐都很友善。
	Zhètiáolǐngdàigènghǎoérqiěbùbǐnàtiáolǐngdàichà 4. 这条领带更好而且不比那条领带差。 This necktie is better than and not inferior to that necktie.
	Nǐbǐwǒqiángzhuàng ma? 5. 你比我强壮吗？ Are you stronger than me?

Exercise 7/liànxíqī – Comparison/yìtóng

Dàwèishìzuìhǎo de duìyuán
6. 大卫是最好的队员。
David is the best player.

Tābǐqítāshāngrénchéngshí de duō.
7. 他比其他商人诚实的多。
He is more honest than any other trader.

Zhègenánháihéwǒyīyàngyǒnggǎn
8. 这个男孩和我一样勇敢。
The boy is as brave as me.

Xīnbùliàobǐlǎobùliàohǎo
9. 新布料比老布料好。
A new cloth is better than an old one.

Zhègerénbǐwǒqiángzhuàng
10.这个人比我强壮。
The man is stronger than me.

Zhìhuìbǐcáifùkěqǔ.

11.智慧比财富可取。

Wisdom is preferable to wealth.

智慧比财富可贵。

Zhègegōngzuòshìbǐyǐqiángèngchà

12.这个工作室比以前更差。

The workshop is worse than before.

Jiànkāngbǐcáifùgèngzhòngyào

13.健康比财富更重要。

Health is more important than wealth.

Lúndūnshìyīngguósuǒyǒuchéngshìzhōng

zuìdà de

14.伦敦是英国所有城市中最大的。

London is the largest of all the UK cities.

伦敦是英国最大的城市。

Zàizhōngbù,

bómínghànbǐqítārènhéchéngshìdūdà.

15.在中部，伯明翰比其他任何城市都大。

Birmingham is larger than any city in the

Midlands.

Wǒrènwéizhèliǎnggèrénzhōngāndélǔwǎn gqiúdǎ de gènghǎoxiē

16.我认为这两个人中安德鲁网球打的更好些。
I think Andrew is better of the two at tennis.

Zhèshìwǒmensuǒkèfú de zuìyánzhòng de dǎjí

17.这是我们所克服的最严重的打击。
This was the severest blow we have ever endured.

Bùjǐntāngmǔliányuēhàndōuméigēnwǒlái

18.不仅汤姆连约翰都没跟我来。
Neither Tom nor John is coming with me.

不论是汤姆还是约翰都没跟我来。

Zhèxiēnánháimenkànshàngqùdōushòugu òlèisì de jiàoyǎng

19.这些男孩们看上去都受过类似的教养。
The boys seemed to be dressed in a similar manner.

Tā de lǐfúbǐwǒángguì.
20.她的礼服比我昂贵。
Her dress is costlier than mine.

她的礼服比我的昂贵。

Zhègenǚháitiàowǔxiàngwǒyīyàng

21. 这个女孩跳舞像我一样。
The girl dances like me.

这个女孩的舞姿跳得像我一样。

Zhèjiādiànbǐnàjiādiàndà

22. 这家店比那家店大。
This shop is larger than that shop.

Mòhǎnmòdéyǐtāzhègeniánlíngsuànshìzuì hǎo de quánjíshǒule.

23. 默罕默德以他这个年龄算是最好的拳击手了。
Muhammad was the greatest boxer of his age.

按默罕默德的年龄段来说，他算是最好的拳击手了。

Zhègeérzizǒulùjiùxiàngtāfùqīn yīyàng.

24. 这个儿子走路就像他父亲一样。
The son walks exactly as the father does.

练习8-教育

Exercise 8/liànxíbā – Education/jiàoxué

	Zhèxiēshūduìxuéshēngyǒuyòngchù 1. 这些书对学生有用处。 These books are useful for the students.
	Qízhōngyīběnshū zhègeshūdiàn li Méiyǒu. 2. 其中一本书这个书店里没有。 One of the books is not available in the bookshop.
	Xiàozhǎngshuōletājīntiānhuìràngxuéxiàokāizh e. 3. 校长说了他今天会让学校开着。 The proprietor said that he would keep the school open today. 校长说了他今天会让学校继续开课。
	Hěnduōxuéshēngcéngjīngbèizhègelǎoshī chéngfáguò 4. 很多学生曾经被这个老师惩罚过。 Many students were punished by the teacher. 很多学生都被这个老师惩罚过。
	Sānniánqiántāzhèngzàilúndūnxuéxí 5. 3年前她正在伦敦学习。 Three years ago she was studying in London.

Hěnduōshūguòqùzhèngtǎngzàizhègejià zishàng

6. 很多书过去正躺在这个架子上。
   Many books were lying on the shelf.

Shùxuéyǐqiánduìyútāéryánshìwúfǎlǐjiě de

7. 数学以前对于她而言是无法理解的。
   Mathematics was not understood by her.

Tàilēixiǎojiěbǎnàbèntāwúfǎyuèdú de shū guīhuánle

8. 泰勒小姐把那本她无法阅读的书归还了。
   Miss Taylor returned the book which she could not read.

   泰勒小姐归还了那本她看不懂的书。

Wǒhuìkàndàojiātíngzuòyèzuòwán de

9. 我会看到家庭作业做完的。
   I will see that the homework is done.

   我会看到做完的家庭作业。

Zhègejiǎngshī de xiāoxicéngjīngshìkǒuyǔ de bùshìshūmiàn de

10. 这个讲师的消息曾经是口语的不是书面的。
    The lecturer's message was verbal not written.

    这个讲师的信息曾经是以口传而不是书面发放的。

Yǐqiánzhèxiēnánháizimenzhōng de

měiyīgèdōufēichángjīngtōngshùxué.

11. 以前这些男孩子们中的每一个都非常精通数学。

Each one of the boys was well versed in

Mathematics.

这些男孩子每一个都非常精通数学。

Tācéngjīngbǎzhuōshàngsuǒyǒu de

shūdōunázǒuliǎo.

12. 她曾经把桌上所有的书都拿走了。

She took away all the books on the table.

她把桌上所有的书都拿走了。

Zhèèrshígèxuéshēngzhōng de

měiyīgèdōucéngbèiyāoqǐngqùguòzhègejùyuàn

13. 这二十个学生中的每一个都曾被邀请去过这个剧院。

Each of the twenty students was invited to the theatre.

这二十个学生都曾被邀请去过这个剧院。

Zhègejiǎngshīcéngduìxuéshēngmenshēnggqì

14. 这个讲师曾对学生们生气。

The lecturer was angry with the students.

Zàikǎoshìzhōngqínfèngōngzuòduìchénggōngshìzhìguānzhòngyào de

15. 在考试中勤奋工作对成功是至关重要的。

Hard work is essential for success in examinations.

用功是考试成功的要诀。

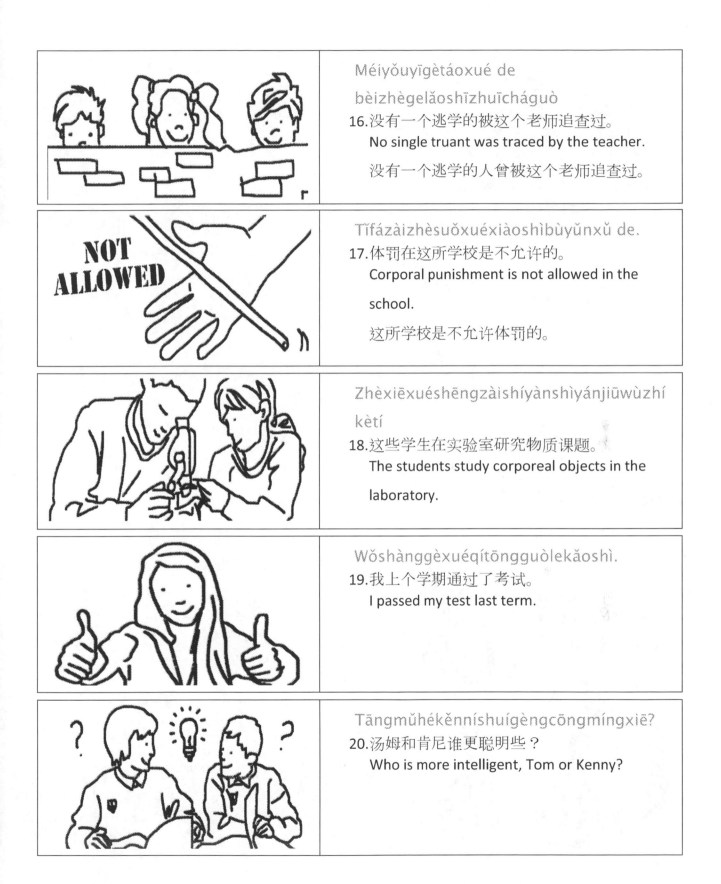

Méiyǒuyīgètáoxué de bèizhègelǎoshīzhuīcháguò

16.没有一个逃学的被这个老师追查过。

No single truant was traced by the teacher.

没有一个逃学的人曾被这个老师追查过。

Tǐfázàizhèsuǒxuéxiàoshìbùyǔnxǔ de.

17.体罚在这所学校是不允许的。

Corporal punishment is not allowed in the school.

这所学校是不允许体罚的。

Zhèxiēxuéshēngzàishíyànshìyánjiūwùzhí kètí

18.这些学生在实验室研究物质课题。

The students study corporeal objects in the laboratory.

Wǒshànggèxuéqítōngguòlekǎoshì.

19.我上个学期通过了考试。

I passed my test last term.

Tāngmǔhékěnníshuígèngcōngmíngxiē?

20.汤姆和肯尼谁更聪明些？

Who is more intelligent, Tom or Kenny?

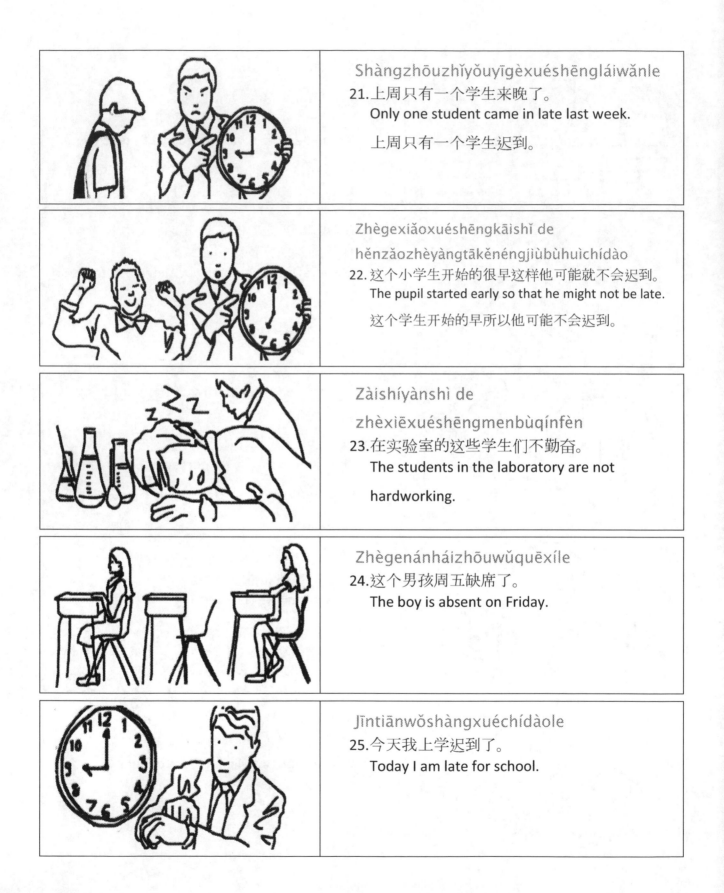

Shàngzhōuzhǐyǒuyīgèxuéshēngláiwǎnle
21. 上周只有一个学生来晚了。
Only one student came in late last week.

上周只有一个学生迟到。

Zhègexiǎoxuéshēngkāishǐ de
hěnzǎozhèyàngtākěnéngjiùbùhuìchídào
22. 这个小学生开始的很早这样他可能就不会迟到。
The pupil started early so that he might not be late.

这个学生开始的早所以他可能不会迟到。

Zàishíyànshì de
zhèxiēxuéshēngmenbùqínfèn
23. 在实验室的这些学生们不勤奋。
The students in the laboratory are not

hardworking.

Zhègenánháizhōuwǔquēxíle
24. 这个男孩周五缺席了。
The boy is absent on Friday.

Jīntiānwǒshàngxuéchídàole
25. 今天我上学迟到了。
Today I am late for school.

Zhègelǎoshīgěilewǒyīxiēhěnhǎo de jiànyì.
26.这个老师给了我一些很好的建议。
The teacher gave me some good advice.

Tāmenzhōng de

měiyīgèdōubèizhègelǎoshībiǎoyángle
27.他们中的每一个都被这个老师表扬了。
Each of them was praised by the teacher.

他们每一个都被这个老师表扬了。

Nǐbìxūshǐzhèxiēnánháixuéxízhèduàn
28.你必须使这些男孩学习这段。
You must make the boys study the passage.

你必须让这些男孩学习这段。

Chúlezhèxiējiǎngshīméiyǒurénbèiyāoqǐn

gcānjiāzhèchūxì
29.除了这些讲师没有人被邀请参加这出戏。
No one was invited for the play except the

lecturers.

Yīxìliè de

jiǎngshīyǐjīngbèizhègedàxuéānpáihǎole
30. 一系列的讲师已经被这个大学安排好了。
A series of lectures has been arranged by the

college.

校方已安排好了一系列的课程。

Zhègebānjíměigènǚháidūhuìjǐntāzuìdà de nǔlì.

31. 这个班级每个女孩都会尽她最大的努力。
Every girl in the class will do her utmost.

Exercise 9/liànxíjiǔ – Recreation/Leisure/ xiāoqiǎn/xiá

	Nánháimenqùgōngyuán 1. 男孩们去公园。 The boys go to the park.
	Bǎoluózàijiālǐhézàigōngyuányīzhítǐnghuópō 2. 保罗在家里和在公园一直挺活泼。 Paul is always playful at home and on the playground.
	Bùjǐndǎoshīmenliánxuéshēngmendōuméichūxíwǔhuì. 3. 不仅导师们连学生们都没出席舞会。 Neither the tutors nor the students were present at the dance.
	Zhègenánháicéngjīngzhājìnlehélǐ. 4. 这个男孩曾经扎进了河里。 The boy plunged into the river.
	Zhèlèi de shūbùyīnggāigěiháizimen 5. 这类的书不应该给孩子们。 Such books ought not to be given to children.

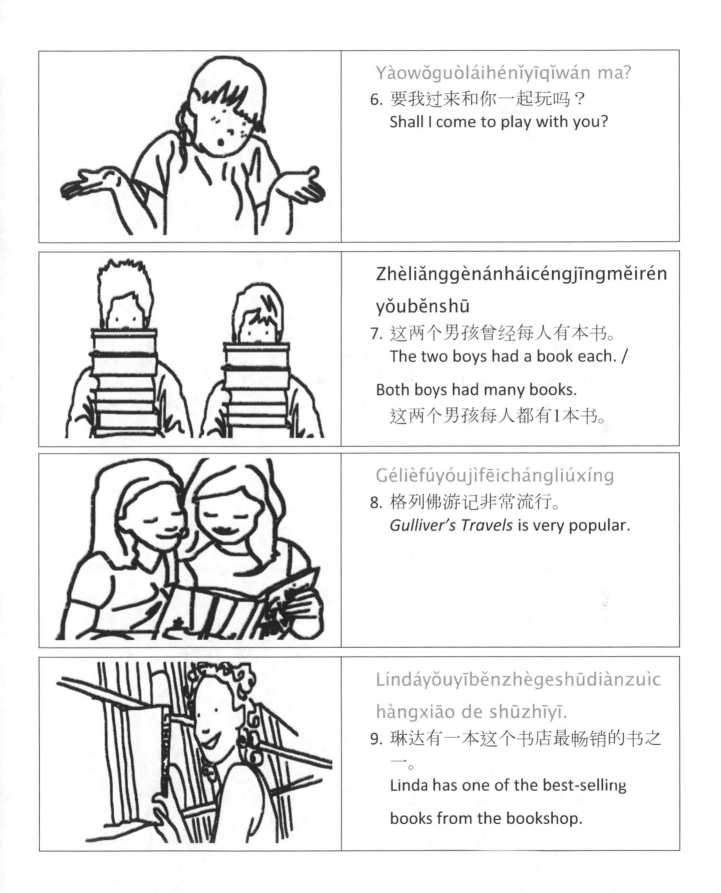

Yàowǒguòláihénǐyīqǐwán ma?

6. 要我过来和你一起玩吗？

Shall I come to play with you?

Zhèliǎnggènánháicéngjīngměirén yǒuběnshū

7. 这两个男孩曾经每人有本书。

The two boys had a book each. /

Both boys had many books.

这两个男孩每人都有1本书。

Gélièfúyóujìfēichángliúxíng

8. 格列佛游记非常流行。

Gulliver's Travels is very popular.

Líndáyǒuyīběnzhègeshūdiànzuìchàngxiāo de shūzhīyī.

9. 琳达有一本这个书店最畅销的书之一。

Linda has one of the best-selling books from the bookshop.

练习10-个人

Exercise 10/liànxíshí – Individual (1ˢᵗ/3ʳᵈ person)/gèrén (rénchēnghuòzhěsānrénkǒuqì)

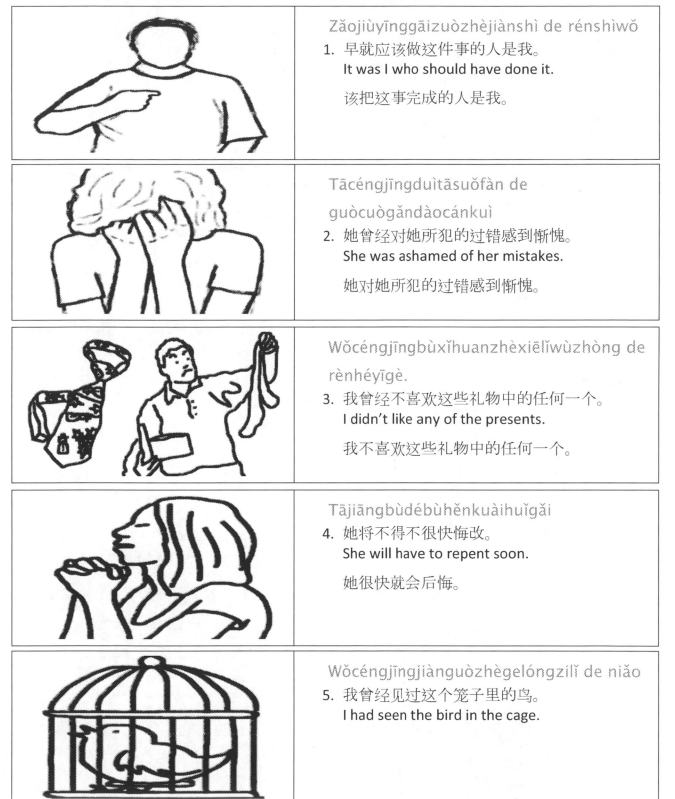

Zǎojiùyīnggāizuòzhèjiànshì de rénshìwǒ
1. 早就应该做这件事的人是我。
   It was I who should have done it.

   该把这事完成的人是我。

Tācéngjīngduìtāsuǒfàn de guòcuògǎndàocánkuì
2. 她曾经对她所犯的过错感到惭愧。
   She was ashamed of her mistakes.

   她对她所犯的过错感到惭愧。

Wǒcéngjīngbùxǐhuanzhèxiēlǐwùzhòng de rènhéyīgè.
3. 我曾经不喜欢这些礼物中的任何一个。
   I didn't like any of the presents.

   我不喜欢这些礼物中的任何一个。

Tājiāngbùdébùhěnkuàihuǐgǎi
4. 她将不得不很快悔改。
   She will have to repent soon.

   她很快就会后悔。

Wǒcéngjīngjiànguòzhègelóngzilǐ de niǎo
5. 我曾经见过这个笼子里的鸟。
   I had seen the bird in the cage.

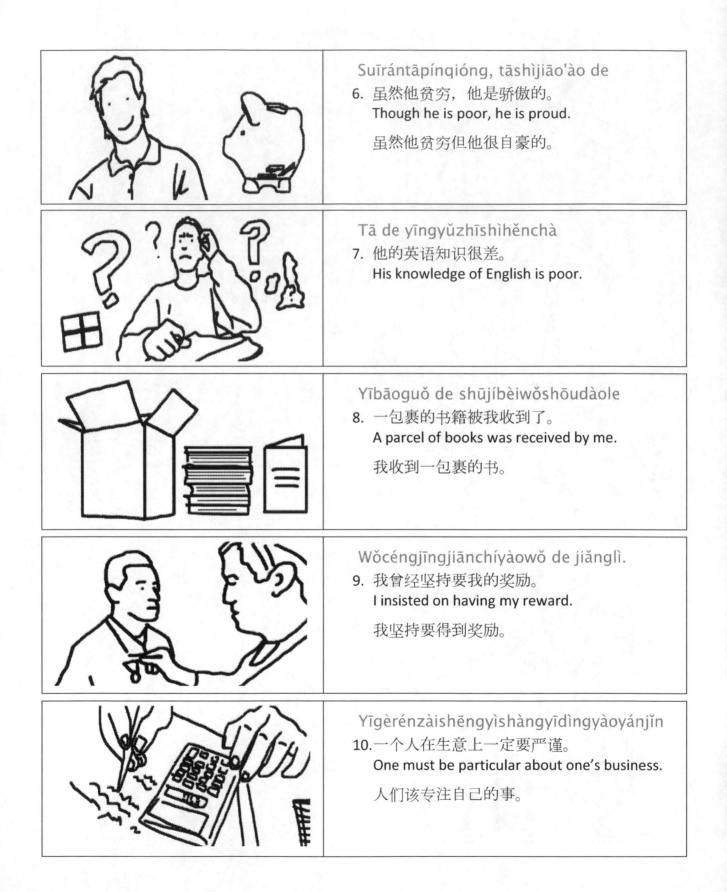

Suīrántāpínqióng, tāshìjiāo'ào de

6. 虽然他贫穷，他是骄傲的。
   Though he is poor, he is proud.

   虽然他贫穷但他很自豪的。

Tā de yīngyǔzhīshìhěnchà

7. 他的英语知识很差。
   His knowledge of English is poor.

Yībāoguǒ de shūjíbèiwǒshōudàole

8. 一包裹的书籍被我收到了。
   A parcel of books was received by me.

   我收到一包裹的书。

Wǒcéngjīngjiānchíyàowǒ de jiǎnglì.

9. 我曾经坚持要我的奖励。
   I insisted on having my reward.

   我坚持要得到奖励。

Yīgèrénzàishēngyìshàngyīdìngyàoyánjǐn

10. 一个人在生意上一定要严谨。
    One must be particular about one's business.

    人们该专注自己的事。

Fălánxīsijǐnjǐnzhuómóchūlewǔgèwèntí

11. 法兰茜丝仅仅琢磨出了5个问题。

Francis has worked out only five problems.

法兰茜丝仅仅琢磨出5个问题。

Yīgèrénkěnéngbiǎoxiàn de jiùxiàngzàizìjǐfángjiānyīyàng.

12.　　一个人可能表现得就像在自己房间一样。

One can behave as one likes in one's own room.

练习11-健康

Exercise 11/liànxíshíyī – Health/yīliáobǎojiàn

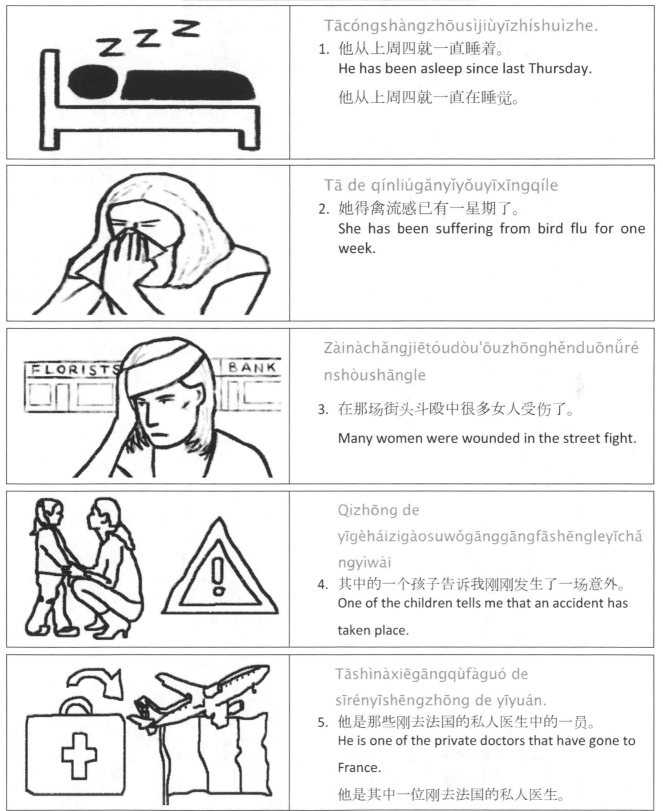

Tācóngshàngzhōusìjiùyīzhíshuìzhe.

1. 他从上周四就一直睡着。
   He has been asleep since last Thursday.

   他从上周四就一直在睡觉。

Tā de qínliúgǎnyǐyǒuyīxīngqíle

2. 她得禽流感已有一星期了。
   She has been suffering from bird flu for one week.

Zàinàchǎngjiētóudòu'ōuzhōnghěnduōnǚré nshòushāngle

3. 在那场街头斗殴中很多女人受伤了。

   Many women were wounded in the street fight.

Qízhōng de yīgèháizigàosuwǒgānggāngfāshēngleyīchǎ ngyìwài

4. 其中的一个孩子告诉我刚刚发生了一场意外。
   One of the children tells me that an accident has

   taken place.

Tāshìnàxiēgāngqùfàguó de sīrényīshēngzhōng de yīyuán.

5. 他是那些刚去法国的私人医生中的一员。
   He is one of the private doctors that have gone to

   France.

   他是其中一位刚去法国的私人医生。

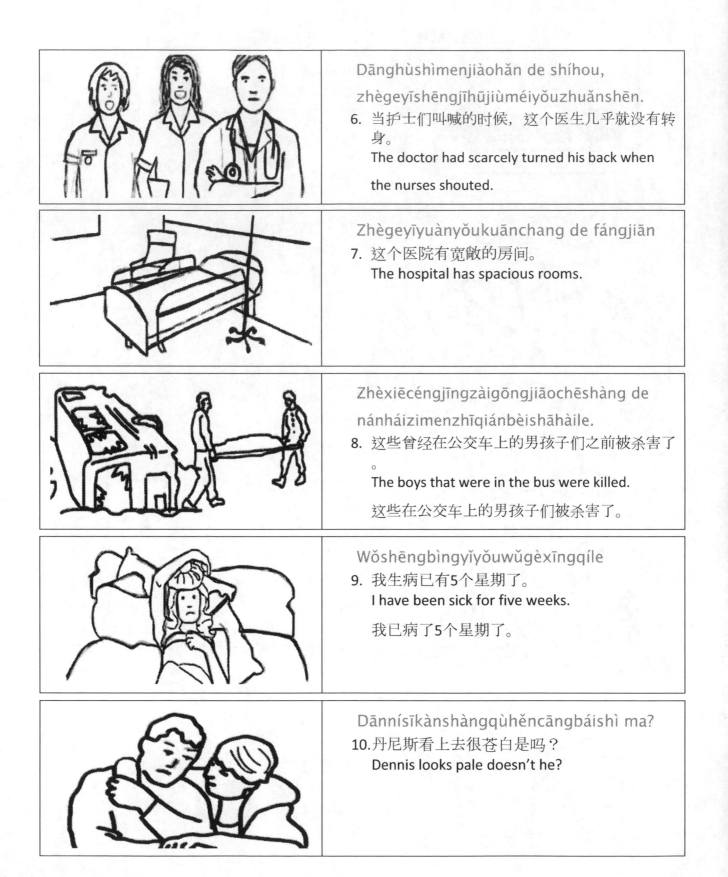

Dānghùshìmenjiàohǎn de shíhou, zhègeyīshēngjīhūjiùméiyǒuzhuǎnshēn.

6. 当护士们叫喊的时候，这个医生几乎就没有转身。
The doctor had scarcely turned his back when the nurses shouted.

Zhègeyīyuànyǒukuānchang de fángjiān

7. 这个医院有宽敞的房间。
The hospital has spacious rooms.

Zhèxiēcéngjīngzàigōngjiāochēshàng de nánháizimenzhīqiánbèishāhàile.

8. 这些曾经在公交车上的男孩子们之前被杀害了。
The boys that were in the bus were killed.

这些在公交车上的男孩子们被杀害了。

Wǒshēngbìngyǐyǒuwǔgèxīngqíle

9. 我生病已有5个星期了。
I have been sick for five weeks.

我已病了5个星期了。

Dānnísīkànshàngqùhěncāngbáishì ma?

10. 丹尼斯看上去很苍白是吗？
Dennis looks pale doesn't he?

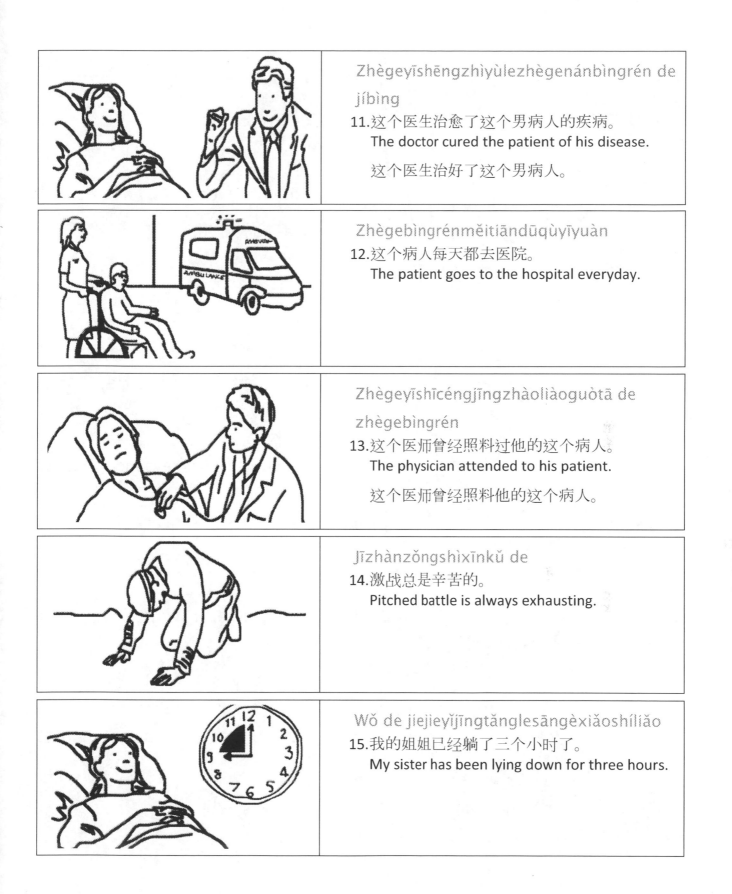

Zhègeyīshēngzhìyùlezhègenánbìngrén de jíbìng

11. 这个医生治愈了这个男病人的疾病。
The doctor cured the patient of his disease.

这个医生治好了这个男病人。

Zhègebìngrénměitiāndūqùyīyuàn

12. 这个病人每天都去医院。
The patient goes to the hospital everyday.

Zhègeyīshīcéngjīngzhàoliàoguòtā de zhègebìngrén

13. 这个医师曾经照料过他的这个病人。
The physician attended to his patient.

这个医师曾经照料他的这个病人。

Jīzhànzǒngshìxīnkǔ de

14. 激战总是辛苦的。
Pitched battle is always exhausting.

Wǒ de jiějieyǐjīngtǎnglesāngèxiǎoshílìǎo

15. 我的姐姐已经躺了三个小时了。
My sister has been lying down for three hours.

Yīgèshòushāngle,
yīgèbèibǔle

16. 一个受伤了，一个被捕
了。
One was wounded, and one
was captured.

Zhègenánhái de
jíbìngshìwúfǎzhìyù de

17. 这个男孩的疾病是无法
治愈的。
The boy's disease is incurable.

Xīnxiānkōngqìyǒulìyúhǎo
de jiànkāng

18. 新鲜空气有利于好的健
康。
Fresh air is conducive to good
health.

练习 12-家庭

Exercise 12/liànxíshí'èr – Family/tiānlún

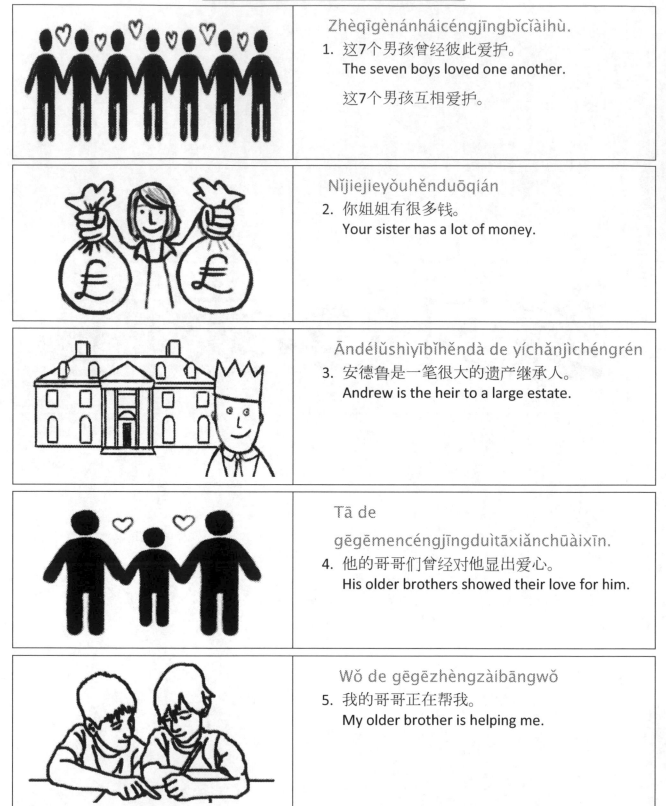

Zhèqīgènánháicéngjīngbǐcǐàihù.

1. 这7个男孩曾经彼此爱护。
   The seven boys loved one another.

   这7个男孩互相爱护。

Nǐjiejieyǒuhěnduōqián

2. 你姐姐有很多钱。
   Your sister has a lot of money.

Āndélǔshìyībǐhěndà de yíchǎnjìchéngrén

3. 安德鲁是一笔很大的遗产继承人。
   Andrew is the heir to a large estate.

Tā de

gēgēmencéngjīngduìtāxiǎnchūàixīn.

4. 他的哥哥们曾经对他显出爱心。
   His older brothers showed their love for him.

Wǒ de gēgēzhèngzàibāngwǒ

5. 我的哥哥正在帮我。
   My older brother is helping me.

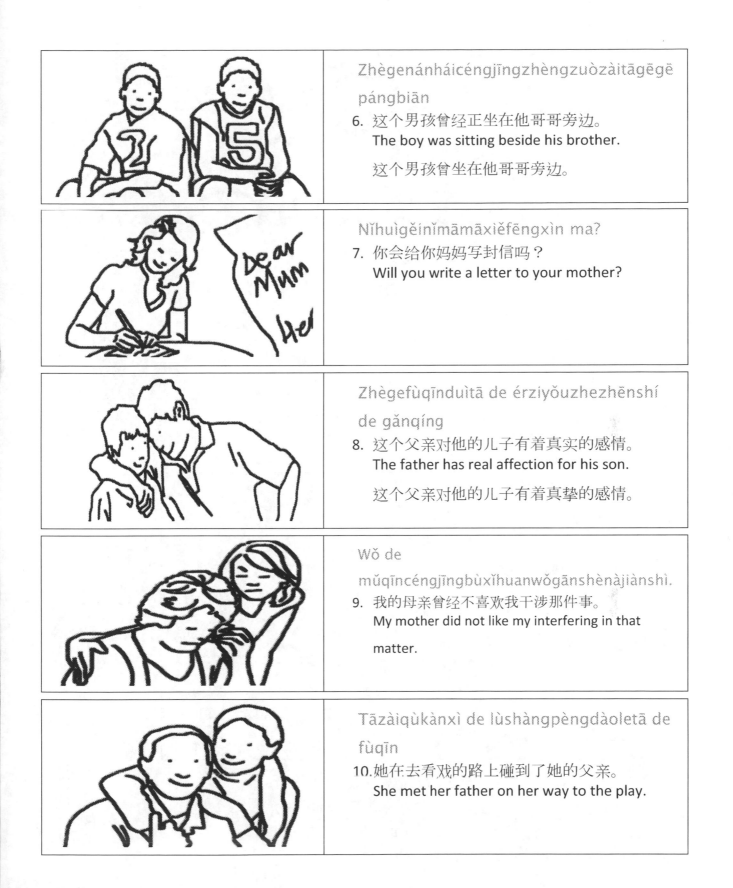

Zhègenánháicéngjīngzhèngzuòzàitāgēgē pángbiān

6. 这个男孩曾经正坐在他哥哥旁边。
   The boy was sitting beside his brother.

   这个男孩曾坐在他哥哥旁边。

Nǐhuìgěinǐmāmāxiěfēngxìn ma?

7. 你会给你妈妈写封信吗？
   Will you write a letter to your mother?

Zhègefùqīnduìtā de érziyǒuzhezhēnshí de gǎnqíng

8. 这个父亲对他的儿子有着真实的感情。
   The father has real affection for his son.

   这个父亲对他的儿子有着真挚的感情。

Wǒ de mǔqīncéngjīngbùxǐhuanwǒgānshènàjiànshì.

9. 我的母亲曾经不喜欢我干涉那件事。
   My mother did not like my interfering in that

   matter.

Tāzàiqùkànxì de lùshàngpèngdàoletā de fùqīn

10. 她在去看戏的路上碰到了她的父亲。
    She met her father on her way to the play.

Zhàngfūmenduìtāmen de qīzimenyǒupiānxīn.

11. 丈夫们对他们的妻子们有偏心。

Husbands have a bias towards their wives.

丈夫们都偏爱自己的妻子。

Yīgèrénbìxūzhuānàitā de qīzi.

12.   一个人必须专爱他的妻子。

One must love one's wife.

练习**13**-对话，社交场合

Exercise 13/liànxíshísān – Conversation/Social Occasion/ huìhuà/shèjiāo

Nǐshénmeshíhouhuíjiā

1. 你什么时候回家？
   When will you go home?

Tāzǎoyǐtóngyìnǐ de jiànyìliǎorújīnyěshì

2. 他早已同意你的建议了如今也是。
   He has agreed and he still agrees to your

   suggestion.

   他早已同意你的建议了，而且仍然如此。

Tācéngjīngbìkǒubùtán

3. 他曾经闭口不谈。
   He spoke no further.

Tāshuōtādìèrtiānhuìhuíjiā de.

4. 她说她第二天会回家的。
   She says that she will go home the following

   day.

Zhèxiēxīnwéncéngjīnglìngrénkǒnghuāng

5. 这些新闻曾经令人恐慌。
   The news was alarming.

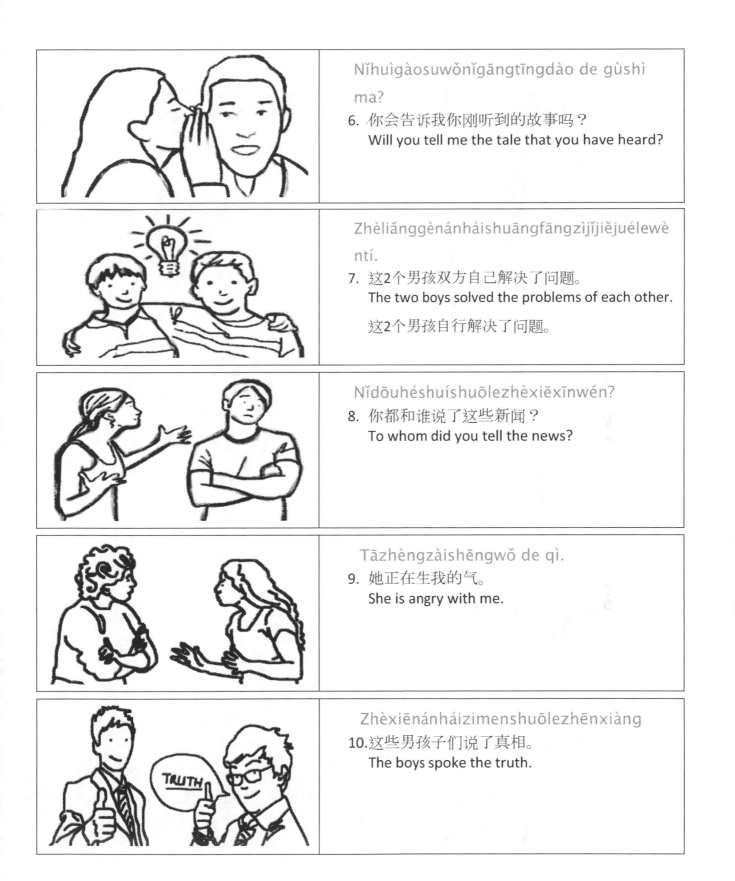

Nǐhuìgàosuwǒnǐgāngtīngdào de gùshì ma?

6. 你会告诉我你刚听到的故事吗？
Will you tell me the tale that you have heard?

Zhèliǎnggènánháishuāngfāngzìjǐjiějuélewènti.

7. 这2个男孩双方自己解决了问题。
The two boys solved the problems of each other.

这2个男孩自行解决了问题。

Nǐdōuhéshuíshuōlezhèxiēxīnwén?

8. 你都和谁说了这些新闻？
To whom did you tell the news?

Tāzhèngzàishēngwǒ de qì.

9. 她正在生我的气。
She is angry with me.

Zhèxiēnánháizimenshuōlezhēnxiàng

10.这些男孩子们说了真相。
The boys spoke the truth.

Wèntíchūzàinǐwǒzhījiān

11. 问题出在你我之间。

This matter is between you and me.

Nǐhéchálǐzhèngdàibiǎozhēzhègezhèn

12. 你和查理正代表着这个镇。

You and Charles are representing the town.

Wǒhěngāoxìng de jiēshòunǐxiàzhōurì de yāoqǐng

13. 我很高兴的接受你下周日的邀请。

I am pleased to accept your invitation for next Sunday.

Nǐyǐqiánwéishén me sāhuǎng?

14. 你以前为什么撒谎？

Why did you lie?

你为什么撒谎？

Wǒmenzhōng de yīgèbìxūqù kāihuì

15. 我们中的一个必须去开会。

One of us must go to the meeting.

我们当中一个必须去开会。

Liǎnggènǚháidōucéngchūxíle
16. 2个女孩都曾出席了。
Both girls were present.

2个女孩都曾出席。

Zhègejuédìngshìzàinǐwǒzhījiān
17. 这个决定是在你我之间。
The decision is between you and me.

这是你我之间的决定。

Rúguǒwǒshìnǐdehuàwǒjiùbùhuìqù
18. 如果我是你的话我就不会去。
I would not go if I were you.

Wǒkěyǐpéinǐqùjùyuàn ma?
19. 我可以陪你去剧院吗？
May I accompany you to the theatre?

Wǒyǒuzhejídà de yuànwàngxiǎngjiànnǐ
20. 我有着极大的愿望想见你。
I have a great desire to meet you.

我切望见到你。

Zhègenánréncéngjīngméiyǒushuōshìshuí

21. 这个男人曾经没有说是谁。
The man did not say who it was.

这个男人没有说是谁。

Nǐduìlǐjiěfǎyǔyǒurènhékùnnán ma?

22. 你对理解法语有任何困难吗？
Do you have any difficulty in understanding French?

你理解法语有任何困难吗？

Nǐshénmeshíhouláiwǒhuāyuán?

23. 你什么时候来我花园？
When will you come to my garden?

你什么时候来我的花园？

Nǐgèngyuànyìhéshuíwán?

24. 你更愿意和谁玩？
Whom would you prefer to play with?

练习14-工作

Exercise 14/liànxíshísì – Work/gōngzuò

Zhègezuòjiācéngjīngzhuānzhùyúwánché

ngzhèběnshū

1. 这个作家曾经专注于完成这本书。
   The Author was bent upon completing the

   book.

Zuótiānzuìhòuyīgèxuétúbèiquèdìngle

2. 昨天最后一个学徒被确定了。
   The last apprentice was admitted yesterday.

   昨天确定了最后一个学徒。

Xīnqín de

gōngzuòjiāshàngzhuānzhùjiùyǐjīngquèbǎoletā de

chénggōng

3. 辛勤的工作加上专注就已经确保了他的成功。
   Hard work in addition to concentration has ensured his

   success.

   勤奋加上专注就是成功的保证。

Tācéngjīngbèizhǐkòngwànhūzhíshǒu

4. 她曾经被指控玩忽职守。
   She was accused of neglect of duty.

Zhèxiēwǔzhěpiān'àikuānsōng de

fúzhuāng

5. 这些舞者偏爱宽松的服装。
   The dancers prefer loose clothes.

Gōngrénjiējíbìxūyàozhǔdǎojiéjiǎn de shēnghuó

6. 工人阶级必须要主导节俭的生活。
The working class must lead an economical life.

工人阶级必须倡导节俭的生活。

Zhègeláogōngbùzàitiánlǐgōngzuò.

7. 这个劳工不在田里工作。
The labourer does not work in the field.

Zhèxiēcéngjīngbèigùyōng de mùjiangzhōng de yīgègānggāngbèijiěgùle

8. 这些曾经被雇佣的木匠中的一个刚刚被解雇了。
One of the carpenters who were employed, has been dismissed from the work.

其中一位被雇佣的木匠刚刚被解雇了。

Zhègetúdìyīnggāifúcóngtā de shīfu

9. 这个徒弟应该服从他的师傅。
The apprentice should obey his master.

Zhègenǚháicéngjīngquánshénguànzhù de gōngzuò

10. 这个女孩曾经全神贯注的工作。
The girl was absorbed in her work.

这个女孩曾经全神贯注地工作。

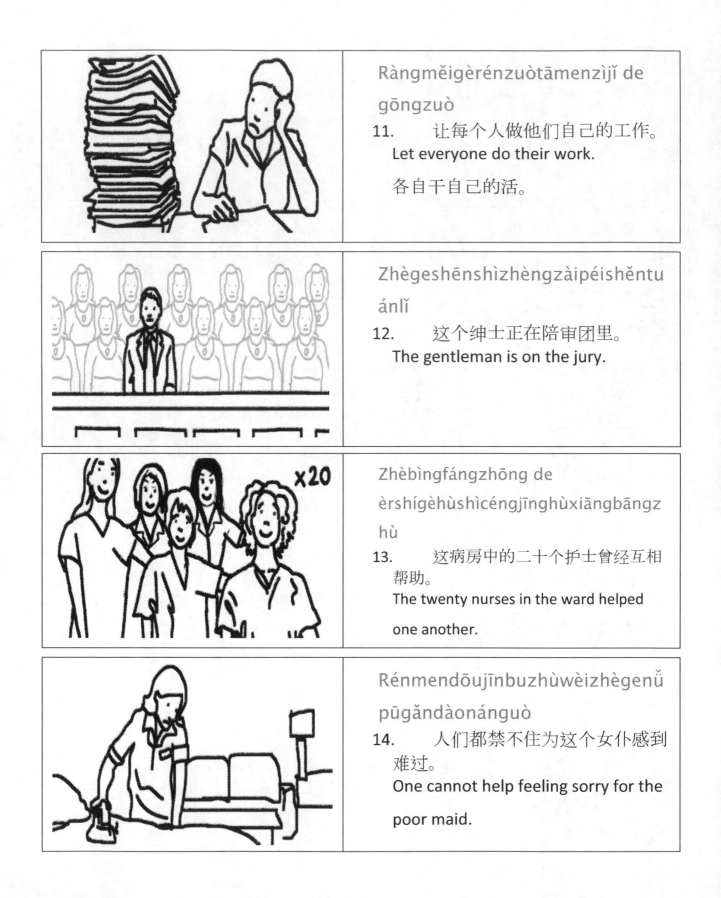

Ràngměigèrénzuòtāmenzìjǐ de gōngzuò

11. 让每个人做他们自己的工作。
Let everyone do their work.

各自干自己的活。

Zhègeshēnshìzhèngzàipéishěntuánlǐ

12. 这个绅士正在陪审团里。
The gentleman is on the jury.

Zhèbìngfángzhōng de èrshígèhùshìcéngjīnghùxiāngbāngzhù

13. 这病房中的二十个护士曾经互相帮助。
The twenty nurses in the ward helped one another.

Rénmendōujīnbuzhùwèizhègenǚpūgǎndàonánguò

14. 人们都禁不住为这个女仆感到难过。
One cannot help feeling sorry for the poor maid.

练习15-事实

Exercise 15/liànxíshíwǔ – Fact/shìshí

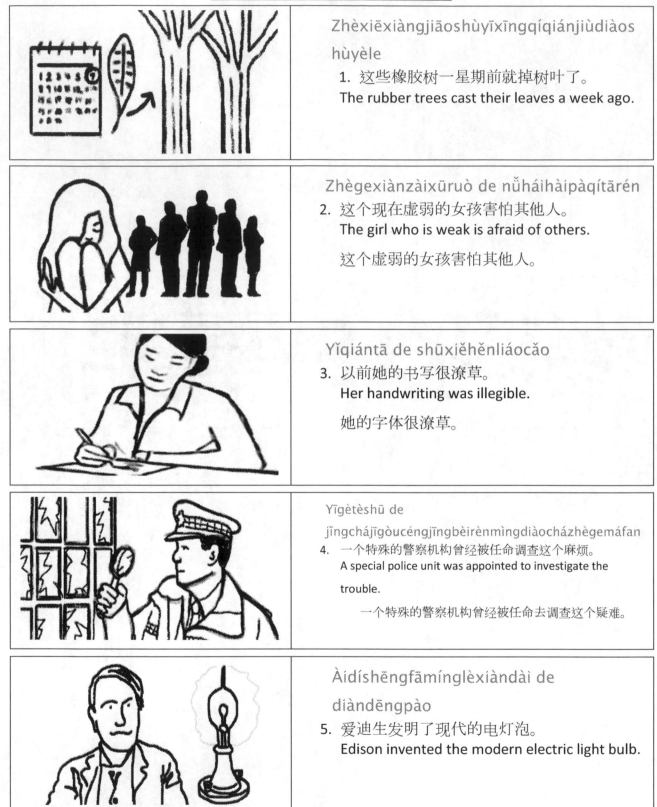

Zhèxiēxiàngjiāoshùyīxīngqíqiánjiùdiàoshùyèle

1. 这些橡胶树一星期前就掉树叶了。
The rubber trees cast their leaves a week ago.

Zhègexiànzàixūruò de nǚháihàipàqítārén

2. 这个现在虚弱的女孩害怕其他人。
The girl who is weak is afraid of others.

这个虚弱的女孩害怕其他人。

Yǐqiántā de shūxiěhěnliáocǎo

3. 以前她的书写很潦草。
Her handwriting was illegible.

她的字体很潦草。

Yīgètèshū de jǐngchájīgòucéngjīngbèirènmìngdiàocházhègemáfan

4. 一个特殊的警察机构曾经被任命调查这个麻烦。
A special police unit was appointed to investigate the trouble.

一个特殊的警察机构曾经被任命去调查这个疑难。

Àidíshēngfāmínglèxiàndài de diàndēngpào

5. 爱迪生发明了现代的电灯泡。
Edison invented the modern electric light bulb.

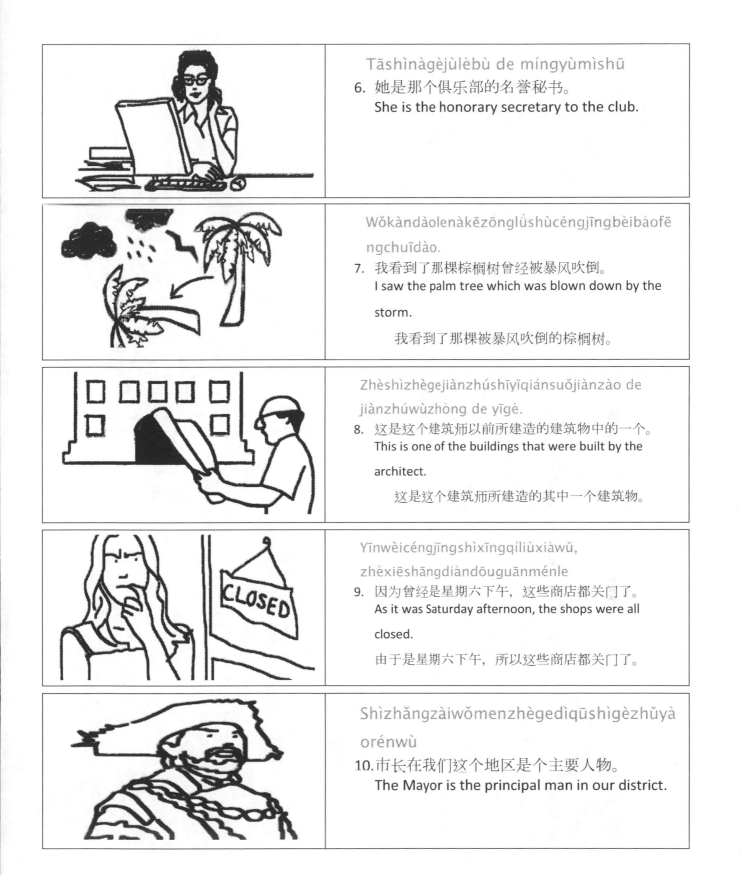

Tāshìnàgèjùlèbù de míngyùmìshū

6. 她是那个俱乐部的名誉秘书。
   She is the honorary secretary to the club.

Wǒkàndàolenàkēzōnglǘshùcéngjīngbèibàofēngchuīdào.

7. 我看到了那棵棕榈树曾经被暴风吹倒。
   I saw the palm tree which was blown down by the storm.

   我看到了那棵被暴风吹倒的棕榈树。

Zhèshìzhègejiànzhúshīyǐqiánsuǒjiànzào de jiànzhúwùzhòng de yīgè.

8. 这是这个建筑师以前所建造的建筑物中的一个。
   This is one of the buildings that were built by the architect.

   这是这个建筑师所建造的其中一个建筑物。

Yīnwèicéngjīngshìxīngqíliùxiàwǔ, zhèxiēshāngdiàndōuguānménle

9. 因为曾经是星期六下午，这些商店都关门了。
   As it was Saturday afternoon, the shops were all closed.

   由于是星期六下午，所以这些商店都关门了。

Shìzhǎngzàiwǒmenzhègedìqūshìgèzhǔyàorénwù

10. 市长在我们这个地区是个主要人物。
    The Mayor is the principal man in our district.

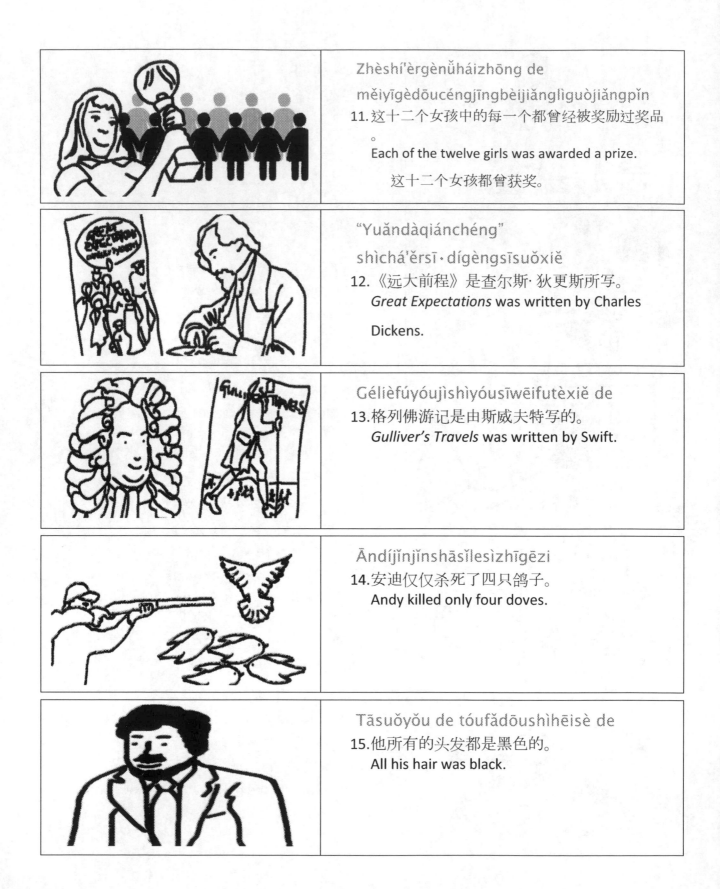

Zhèshí'èrgènǚháizhōng de
mĕiyīgèdōucéngjīngbèijiănglìguòjiăngpĭn

11. 这十二个女孩中的每一个都曾经被奖励过奖品。

Each of the twelve girls was awarded a prize.

这十二个女孩都曾获奖。

"Yuăndàqiánchéng"
shìchá'ěrsī·dígèngsīsuŏxiě

12. 《远大前程》是查尔斯·狄更斯所写。

Great Expectations was written by Charles Dickens.

Gélièfúyóujìshìyóusīwēifutèxiě de

13. 格列佛游记是由斯威夫特写的。

Gulliver's Travels was written by Swift.

Āndíjĭnjĭnshāsĭlesìzhīgēzi

14. 安迪仅仅杀死了四只鸽子。

Andy killed only four doves.

Tāsuŏyŏu de tóufădōushìhēisè de

15. 他所有的头发都是黑色的。

All his hair was black.